# Introduction

World War II began in September 1939 and ended in 1945. The war started in Europe when the German leader, Adolf Hitler, invaded Poland. Within a week Britain, Australia, New Zealand, South Africa, Canada and France had all declared war on Germany. Many other countries joined the fighting during the six years of the war. Over 55 million people died in the war. Many died in concentration camps. Bombs dropped in air raids also killed many other people.

The war ended when the USA dropped two atomic bombs on Japanese cities. After the war, the leaders of countries all around the world were determined to work for peace. They set up a new organisation called the United Nations to try to prevent more wars in the future.

The pictures on page 5 show:
  Poster advertising 1936 Olympic Games in Berlin
  Cover of British *Coronation Song Book*, 1937
  Cover of *Mickey Mouse Annual*
  Newspaper seller on the day Britain declared war,
    September 3, 1939

The pictures on page 6 show:
  Winston Churchill, the British Prime Minister
  The pilot of an RAF bomber plane
  Nazi tanks stuck in the mud in Russia
  Japanese officials surrendering on the American
    warship *Missouri* at the end of the war

# Contents

# 1933

Jan 30     **Hitler becomes Chancellor of Germany**
Feb 28     **Fire destroys German parliament**
March 20    **Concentration camps in Germany**

## New leader for Germany

**January 30, Berlin, Germany** The new leader of Germany is Adolf Hitler. Hitler is also leader of the Nazi party. The Nazis are enemies of the Communists and Jewish people. Many people are afraid that Hitler will now try to destroy these people.

△ Hitler (centre) with his ministers

## Fire burns down German parliament

**February 28, Berlin, Germany** Fire burnt down the German parliament building last night. The parliament building is called the Reichstag. Chancellor Hitler has blamed the Communists for the fire.

## Concentration camps

**March 20, Berlin, Germany** Places called concentration camps are planned in Germany. Anyone who speaks out against the Nazi government will be put in one of these camps. The first camp has already opened at Dachau.

## Countries walk out of League

**October 14, Geneva, Switzerland** Germany and Japan have walked out of the League of Nations. The League of Nations is an international organisation. It was set up after World War I to try to settle arguments in a peaceful way. But many people now think that the League does not have the power to keep the world at peace.

# 1934

## Austrian Chancellor is killed

**July 25, Vienna, Austria** The Austrian leader, Chancellor Dollfuss, was killed today. At noon, armed men went into the offices of Dr Dollfuss and shot him. They would not let a doctor in to see him and he bled to death. The armed men were members of the Austrian Nazi party.

The German leader, Adolf Hitler, has said that the German Nazi party had nothing to do with the killing. But many people think that Hitler had something to do with this crime.

▽ The body of the Austrian Chancellor, Dr Dollfuss, is guarded by two soldiers.

## Leading Nazis killed

**June 30, Munich, Germany** A leading Nazi, Ernst Roehm, has been killed. Some people think that other members of the Nazi party have also died elsewhere in Germany. It seems that Hitler himself ordered the murder of these people.

△ Adolf Hitler with some of his Nazi supporters

# News in brief . . .

## German children become Nazis

**Germany** When German boys are ten years old, they have to join the Young Peoples' Movement. They wear Nazi uniforms and learn to parade like soldiers. When they join the Movement they have to stand under a Nazi flag and say: "Under this flag, I swear to give all my strength to Adolf

△ German boys in the Young Peoples' Movement

Hitler, the man who saved our country. I am willing and ready to die for him, so help me God."

## A German greeting

**Germany** The Nazi government has ordered all Germans to greet each other in a new way. When two people meet they must hold up their right arms and say "Heil Hitler!" which means "Hail, Hitler!".

## Shorts at Wimbledon

**May, London, England** Women tennis players will be allowed to wear shorts instead of skirts at Wimbledon this year. Many male officials are

△ Women tennis players wearing shorts

upset by this new rule. They say that shorts are unsuitable for women to wear. They think that women who play at Wimbledon should set a good example.

## Dillinger dead

**July 22, Chicago, USA** The bank robber and murderer, John Dillinger, is dead. John Dillinger has killed 16 people. The police shot him as he came out of a cinema.

▽ John Dillinger, the bank robber and murderer

## *Queen Mary* launched

**September 26, Glasgow, Scotland** The ship called the *Queen Mary* was launched today. The *Queen Mary* is the first ship ever to weigh more than 75,000 tonnes.

▽ The launch of the *Queen Mary*

# 1935

## Hitler tears up treaty

**March 16, Berlin, Germany** Hitler has torn up the Versailles Treaty. This was the agreement that ended World War I. The Treaty said that Germany could have a small army and navy, and no airforce. Now Hitler has ignored the treaty and started to build up Germany's armed forces.

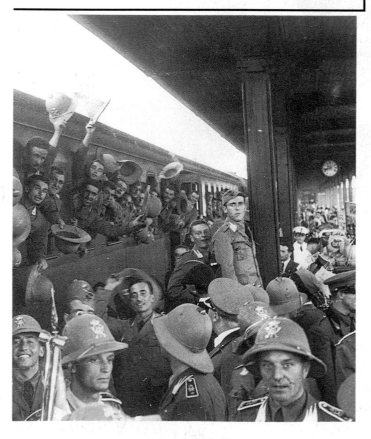

△ Italian troops leave for East Africa.

## War in East Africa

**May, East Africa** It seems likely that there will be a war in East Africa. The Italian leader, Mussolini, has sent troops to Italian East Africa. They are now on the border between East Africa and Abyssinia.

△ The Abyssinian army gets ready for war.

## Italy invades Abyssinia

**October 3, East Africa** Italian troops crossed the border into Abyssinia this morning. The Italians have modern weapons. Many of the Abyssinians only have spears and bows and arrows to fight with.

# News in brief . . .

## Dust storms in America

**April 15, USA** Strong winds have blown clouds of dust across farmland in America (see right). The dust has ruined many crops. Thousands of people have left their homes because they cannot grow any food.

## Good books for everyone

**July, London** Penguin books are in the shops. 'Penguin' is the name of a new family of books published by Mr Allen Lane. The books are paperbacks. They cost only sixpence (two new pence) each.

## Nazis ban jazz music

**October, Berlin** The Nazis have banned all jazz music played by black people or Jewish people in Germany. The Nazis say that this jazz music has a bad effect on young Germans.

## A new world record

**September 3, Bonneville Salt Flats, Utah, USA** Sir Malcolm Campbell has set a new world record for the fastest speed on land. He went at 301 miles (484 kms) per hour in his car *Bluebird*. This is the eighth time Campbell has broken the world record.

## First performance of *Porgy and Bess*

**September 30, Boston, USA** The opera *Porgy and Bess* has its first performance today. *Porgy and Bess* is by George Gershwin. There are many fine tunes in the opera, including the song *Summertime*.

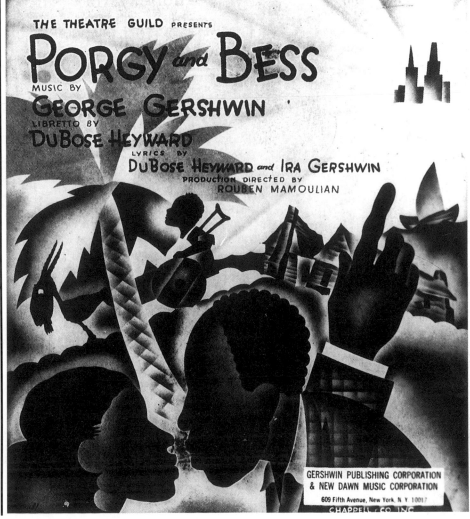

# 1936

## New king for Britain

**January 20, London, England** King George V has died. He had been on the throne for 25 years. The king's eldest son, Edward, becomes King Edward VIII.

▽ A poster showing the power of American industry

## Roosevelt wins again

**November 3, Washington, USA** The American people have elected Franklin D. Roosevelt to be their president for the second time. Roosevelt has been president since 1933. He is very popular with the American people.

## A king in love

**December 10, London, England** The new king is in love with Mrs Wallis Simpson. She is an American who has been married twice before. The king is not allowed to marry someone who has been married before. So King Edward VIII has decided to abdicate. This means that he has given up the throne. His brother will become the new king instead.

Many people have tried to persuade King Edward to leave Mrs Simpson. But he will not change his mind. He has chosen to give up the throne in order to marry Mrs Simpson.

## The new royal family

**December 12, London, England** King Edward VIII has left the country. His new title is the Duke of Windsor. His brother is now the new King George VI. King George and his wife Queen Elizabeth have two daughters, Princess Elizabeth and Princess Margaret. Princess Elizabeth is ten years old.

# Civil war in Spain

**SPANISH CIVIL WAR (July/August 1936)**

Legend:
- Initial advance of Nationalists
- Nationalist territory
- Republican territory

**July 31, Spain** A civil war has started in Spain. A civil war is when people from the same country fight against each other. The Spanish army has attacked the Spanish government and its supporters. The leader of the Spanish army is General Franco. He says that the government is turning Spain into a Communist country. He has started a new political party to fight against Communism. It is called the Nationalist party.

People who are on the side of the Spanish government are called Republicans. The Republicans have formed an army of their own. But the Republican army does not have as many weapons as Franco's army. Fighting between the Republicans and the Nationalists is going on all over Spain.

# Italy occupies Abyssinia

**May 9, Abyssinia** Italian soldiers have reached Addis Ababa, the capital of Abyssinia. The Italians are in control of Addis Ababa. This means that the country of Abyssinia now belongs to Italy. The emperor of Abyssinia has escaped and gone abroad. The king of Italy will now be called 'Emperor of Abyssinia'.

# German troops enter Rhineland

**March 6, Rhineland** German soldiers have gone into the Rhineland. The Rhineland is an area of land between France and Germany. After World War I this area was used to keep the two countries apart. There were to be no troops in this area. People are very unhappy that the German troops have ignored this agreement. Now many people think that Germany wants to start another war.

△ Republican fighters in Barcelona

# News in brief . . .

## A new car for Germany

**February 26, Wolfsburg, Germany** Hitler has opened a new factory in Wolfsburg. The factory will make a cheap family car. This car will be called 'The People's Car'. Its German name is *Volkswagen*.

▷ The new German car, the *Volkswagen*

## Jesse Owens wins medals

**August 15, Berlin, Germany** The eleventh Olympic Games ended today. The black American runner, Jesse Owens, won four gold medals. The Nazis are very angry about this. The Nazis say that white people are better than black people. But a black runner has shown everyone that he is the best in the world.

▽ Jesse Owens

OLYMPIAN ⬡⬡⬡
USA 25
JESSE OWENS 1936

## King Edward's speech

**December 11, London, England** Edward VIII made his last speech as king this evening. The speech was broadcast on the radio. This is part of what he said: "I want you to understand that in making up my mind I did not forget the country or the Empire which as Prince of Wales and lately as king, I have for 25 years tried to serve. But you must believe me when I tell you that I have found it impossible to carry the heavy bur-

△ King Edward makes his last speech.

den of responsibility and to discharge my duties as king as I would wish to do without the help and support of the woman I love . . ."

# 1937

## Fighting in Spain

**February, Spain**   People from other countries are fighting in the Civil War in Spain. Italian and German troops are helping General Franco and the Nationalists. The Russians are helping the Republicans.

## Guernica bombed

**April 26, northern Spain**   This is how a reporter described what he found in the city of Guernica after the German bombing:

'In the Plaza, surrounded almost by a wall of fire, were about a hundred refugees. They were wailing and weeping and rocking to and fro. One middle-aged man spoke English. He told me, "At four, before the market closed, many aeroplanes came. They dropped bombs. Some came low and shot bullets into the streets. . .".'

(Noel Monks, *Eyewitness*, Frederick Muller 1955)

## Spanish city destroyed

**April 30, northern Spain**   Bombs have destroyed the city of Guernica (see map page 13). Guernica is in part of northern Spain held by the Republicans. The bombs were dropped by German planes. The Germans are fighting on the side of General Franco and the Nationalists.

It was market day in Guernica when the Germans dropped the bombs. Fires and explosions killed over 2000 people in Guernica. The people had no warning that the Germans were going to attack. People all round the world are shocked and angry about the bombing.

## George VI crowned

**May 12, London, England**   King George and Queen Elizabeth were crowned this morning in Westminster Abbey. The king and queen's two daughters watched the crowning. Afterwards the royal family went back to Buckingham Palace and waved from the balcony to the huge crowds below.

# News in brief . . .

## Giant airship explodes

**May 6, Lakehurst Airfield, USA** The giant airship *Hindenburg* has exploded. The German airship had just crossed the Atlantic Ocean. It was about to stop at its mooring mast. Suddenly the airship caught fire and the gas inside the airship exploded. All 34 people on board died in the flames.

Only last year the *Hindenburg* had set a new record for the fastest crossing of the Atlantic. It had crossed the ocean in under two days. The Germans were hoping to start a regular passenger service across the Atlantic Ocean.

## The terror of war

**October, Paris, France** The Spanish artist, Pablo Picasso, has painted a picture in protest at the bombing of Guernica earlier this year. His picture reminds people of the terror of war.

▷ Picasso's painting, *Guernica*

## New boxing champion

**June 3, New York, USA** The American boxer, Joe Louis (see right), is the new heavyweight boxing champion of the world. Joe Louis is the first black boxer to be champion for 22 years.

# 1938

March 14      German troops invade Austria
September 27      Hitler threatens war
September 30      Munich meeting
November 11      Germans attack Jews

## Hitler threatens war

**September 27, Germany** Adolf Hitler wants parts of Czechoslovakia to become part of Germany. The British Prime Minister, Neville Chamberlain, has gone to Munich to try to persuade Hitler not to go to war.

△ A picture of Adolf Hitler on a German poster

△ Prime Minister Neville Chamberlain (right) with Adolf Hitler

## Churchill says, "Don't give in"

**September 28, London, England** A member of the British parliament, Winston Churchill, has said that Chamberlain should not give in to Hitler. He says that Britain and France should fight if Germany attacks Czechoslovakia. Many people agree with Winston Churchill.

△ Preparing for war in London. Sandbags protect a police station against bombs.

## Chamberlain returns from Munich

△ Neville Chamberlain returns from Munich.

**September 30, London, England** Crowds of people welcomed Prime Minister Chamberlain as he came back from Munich this evening. Chamberlain waved a piece of paper signed by Hitler and himself. He said that Britain and Germany would not go to war. "It is peace for our time," he said.

The leaders of France, Italy and Britain have agreed that Germany can take over parts of Czechoslovakia. In return, Hitler has said that he will leave the Czech people in peace. Many people are relieved because a war now looks unlikely. But the Czech people are unhappy about this agreement.

## German troops invade Austria

**March 14, Vienna, Austria** German troops have crossed into Austria. People cheered as Hitler drove through the streets of Vienna, the Austrian capital.

The Austrian leader, Seyss Inquart, is a member of the Nazi party. He invited the Germans to invade Austria. Many Austrians would like their country to become part of Germany.

Germany is now the most powerful country in Europe.

# Germans attack Austrian Jews

**March 18, Vienna, Austria**  The Germans have attacked the Jews living in Austria. The Germans have said that no Jewish person is allowed to be a lawyer, doctor or teacher.

△ The Nazis have smashed the windows of shops owned by Jews.

# Danger of war over Czechoslovakia

**May 20, Prague, Czechoslovakia**  Once again, there is a threat of war. German troops now surround Czechoslovakia on three sides (see map). There are many Germans living in Czechoslovakia. They say that the Czech people treat them badly. They have asked Germany for protection.

If Germany does invade Czechoslovakia it will break the agreement made between Chamberlain and Hitler. It is hard to see how Britain and France could avoid going to war against Germany if this happens.

# Franco winning Spanish war

**April 15, Spain**  General Franco claims that he is winning the Spanish Civil War. It seems that the Republicans must face defeat.

# 'Kristallnacht'

**November 11, Berlin, Germany**  Two nights ago mobs attacked Jews all over Germany. Thousands of Jewish shops were smashed and robbed. There was so much broken glass on the streets that the Germans have called it "Kristallnacht" – 'the night of broken glass'.

**GERMANY ATTACKS CZECHOSLOVAKIA**

German-speaking areas of Czechoslovakia

# News in brief . . .

## Snow White success

**January, Hollywood, USA**
Walt Disney's new film *Snow White and the Seven Dwarfs* is a great success. *Snow White* is the first full-length cartoon film to be made.

## Italy wins World Cup

**June 19, Paris, France** The Italian football team has won the World Cup in the final in Paris.

## Britain orders more planes

**July 15, London, England** The British government has ordered 1000 new planes for the Royal Air Force. The planes are called Spitfires.

▽ A Spitfire plane

## British get gas masks

**September 20, London, England** Everyone in Britain is to get a free gas mask. The masks are to protect against poison gas from bombs.

▽ Children carry their new gas masks.

# 1939

March 15     Germany invades Czechoslovakia
March 31     Hitler threatens Poland
August 23    Russia and Germany sign agreement
September 1  Germany invades Poland
September 3  Britain and France declare war on
             Germany

# Hitler invades Czechoslovakia

**March 15, Berlin, Germany** Hitler has invaded Czechoslovakia. Two days ago he sent a list of demands to the Czech government. The Czechs did not give in to Hitler's demands. So Hitler has used this as an excuse to move troops into Czechoslovakia.

△ Germans cheer as Hitler returns to Berlin after the invasion of Czechoslovakia.

# Czech people weep as Germans enter Prague

**March 16, Prague, Czechoslovakia** Czechs showed their anger as the Germans entered their capital city, Prague, today. Some people stood silently, some hissed and booed, some shook their fists. Some wept to see the hated enemy in their country. The German soldiers forced the people to give the Nazi salute. All cafés, restaurants, theatres and cinemas are to be closed.

△ People in Prague are forced to salute like Nazis.

## Czech invasion shocks the world

**March 17** Hitler's invasion of Czechoslovakia has shocked the whole world. Only six months ago, Hitler promised in Munich to leave Czechoslovakia alone. Now he has made the country part of Germany. Both the British and French governments have sent letters to Berlin protesting about the hostile German invasion.

# Russia and Germany sign agreement

**August 23, Moscow, USSR** Russia and Germany have signed an agreement not to go to war against each other. This is bad news for Britain and France. If necessary, they were hoping to persuade Russia to join them against Germany.

**POLAND ATTACKED**

N

Danzig

EAST PRUSSIA

USSR

Warsaw

POLAND

GERMANY

→ German and Russian attacks

Polish Corridor - a narrow strip of land which is Poland's route or 'corridor' to the sea

0 km 250

# Hitler threatens Poland

**March 31, Berlin, Germany** Hitler is now threatening Poland. He wants the Poles to give up the city of Danzig to Germany. Danzig used to be a German city. But it became part of Poland after World War I. Now Hitler wants the city back.

Britain and France have promised to help Poland if Germany attacks.

The PEOPLE'S DISPENSARY FOR SICK ANIMALS OF THE POOR. Inc.

GAS PROOF SHELTER

—FOR—

DOGS. CATS & OTHER SMALL ANIMALS

△ A shelter for animals to protect them from gas in an air raid

# Europe gets ready for war

**August 31, London, England** Europe is getting ready for war. In Poland, France and Britain thousands of young men have left their jobs to join the armed forces.

# Germany invades Poland

**September 1, Poland** German troops invaded Poland early this morning. They pulled down barriers along the border and crossed into Poland.

# Russia attacks Poland

**September 17, Poland** Russian troops have invaded Poland. They are trying to occupy as much of the country as they can before the Germans get there. The Polish army is trapped between the two invaders.

# Britain and France go to war

**September 3, London, England** Britain and France are at war with Germany. Prime Minister Chamberlain gave the news to the British people in a radio broadcast at 11.15 this morning.

# British troops land in France

**September 27, France** About 150,000 troops have landed in France. They will help the French to fight against the Germans.

**EUROPE IN 1939**

ATLANTIC OCEAN

North Sea

FINLAND

NORWAY
SWEDEN
ESTONIA
LATVIA
LITHUANIA

DENMARK

IRELAND
UK
NETH.
BELGIUM
LUX.
FRANCE
SWITZ.
PORTUGAL
SPAIN

GERMANY
E. PRUSSIA
USSR
POLAND
CZECHOSLOVAKIA
AUSTRIA
HUNGARY
ROMANIA
YUGOSLAVIA
ITALY
ALBANIA
BULGARIA
GREECE
TURKEY

Mediterranean Sea

0   km   500

Rhineland

Maginot Line
- a series of forts and underground tunnels built by the French to protect their border with Germany

# Spanish Civil War ends

**March 28, Madrid, Spain** General Franco has won the Civil War in Spain. He has beaten the Republicans and the war is over. But there are many problems for Franco. The war destroyed many towns and cities as well as factories. Many farm animals died. The whole country needs rebuilding, but Spain is now a poor country.

# British children moved to safety

**September 2, London, England** Many British children from the towns and cities are moving to the safety of the countryside. The children are leaving their homes to stay with families in the countryside. This is because the Germans are likely to bomb the cities. The countryside is safer.

# German battleship sinks

**December 17, Montevideo, Uruguay** The German battleship, the *Graf Spee*, has sunk. Her own crew blew the ship up. This is because British warships were waiting for the *Graf Spee* as she left the harbour in Montevideo. There was no escape for the German ship. The Royal Navy has been looking for the *Graf Spee* for weeks.

# Children moved from London

**September 1, London, England** Moving people away from a dangerous place to a safer place is called evacuation. This is a description of the evacuation of some children from a school in London: 'I watched the schoolteachers calling out their names and tying luggage labels on their coats, checking their parcels to see there were warm and clean clothes . . . mothers and fathers were saying goodbye, straightening the girls' hair, getting the boys to blow their noses and lightly and quickly kissing them . . . There was quite a long wait before this small army got its orders . . . to move off . . .

Labelled and lined up the children began to move out of the school.'

(Hilde Marchant, *Women and Children Last*, published by Victor Gollancz Ltd, 1941)

# 1940

May 10    **Churchill new British leader**
May 13    **Germans advance into France**
June 4    **Rescue from Dunkirk**
June 19    **Germans enter Paris**
August 20    **Battle of Britain**

## German invasions

**May 10, Oslo, Norway** German troops invaded Norway and Denmark in April. The Germans took the Danes by surprise. The Danes were not ready to fight so they surrendered to the Germans. There was fighting in Oslo, the Norwegian capital. But a Norwegian Nazi called Quisling took control of the country for the Germans. Now most of Norway is controlled by the Germans. British and French troops have landed in Norway to try to drive the Germans out. But so far they have not succeeded.

## New leader for Britain

**May 10, London, England** Winston Churchill has replaced Neville Chamberlain as leader of Britain. Many people blame Neville Chamberlain for Britain's failure to save Norway from the Germans. Winston Churchill will form a National Government made up of people from all political parties.

## German advances continue

**May 13, France** German troops are still advancing across Europe. They have invaded Holland, Luxembourg and Belgium. Germany is now attacking France. Britain and France are now making plans to fight back.

By 1940 the Germans had taken much of Europe.

# British army trapped in Dunkirk

**May 29, France** German forces have reached the French coast along the Channel. The British army is trapped in the port of Dunkirk. The only way out is by sea.

# Cave discovery

**November 1, Lascaux, France** Some French boys have made an amazing discovery. They were catching rabbits when they saw a gap in some rocks. They went through the gap and found a cave. Paintings covered the cave walls. Experts say that the paintings are 15,000 years old.

# Rescue from Dunkirk

**June 4, London, England** Hundreds of little ships have gone to the rescue of the British army. The ships sailed across the Channel to Dunkirk. They brought back over 300,000 British troops to Britain.

△ British troops waiting at Dunkirk

▽ Cave paintings in Lascaux

# Paris falls to Germans

**June 19, London, England** The Germans have occupied Paris. The Germans now control much of France. But some French people are determined to go on fighting against the Germans. This movement against the Germans is called the Resistance. The Resistance is led by General Charles de Gaulle from London.

# RAF is unbeaten

**August 20, London, England** The Royal Air Force (RAF) is fighting a fierce war against the German airforce (the Luftwaffe). German troops are waiting to invade Britain. But they must wait until the Luftwaffe has destroyed the British defences.

# RAF saves Britain

**September 19, London, England** The RAF says it shot down 185 Luftwaffe planes in air battles on September 15. The RAF seems to have beaten the Luftwaffe in the 'Battle of Britain'. Hitler has given up his plans to invade Britain. The RAF has saved Britain.

△ A painting called *The Battle of Britain* by Paul Nash

# News in brief . . .

## Roosevelt wins again

**November 5, Washington, USA** Once again, Americans have voted for Franklin D. Roosevelt to be their president. This is the third time that Roosevelt has been elected. This is good news for Britain because Roosevelt is a strong supporter of its war efforts.

## Children go home

**January 30, London, England** When the war started last September many children from the cities went to live in the countryside. People thought it would be safer there. But many children did not like living in the countryside. They missed their parents. So many have now gone home, back to the cities.

## Tragedy in the Atlantic

**September 22, London, England** There has been a tragedy in the Atlantic Ocean. The ship *City of Benares* was sailing to America to take many children away from the dangers of war in Britain. But a German submarine sunk the *City of Benares*. Ships have picked up 46 children, but 306 have drowned.

## Pets at war

"Send your pets to the country if you can. If you cannot, remember that your dog will not be allowed to go into a public air raid shelter with you. So don't take him shopping with you. Take him for walks near home, so that you can get back quickly.

Cats can take care of themselves far better than you can. Your cat will probably meet you when you get into the shelter."

(BBC broadcast on how to look after your pets during wartime.)

## Nights underground

**September 30, London, England** Thousands of people in London spend their nights in Underground stations. They

△ People sleeping in the Underground

are sheltering from the German air raids. But the Underground stations are very dirty, as this girl describes:

"Dirt abounds everywhere. The floors are never swept and are filthy. People are sleeping on piles of rubbish."

## The Great Dictator

**November 11, London, England** *The Great Dictator* is a new film by Charlie Chaplin. The film makes fun of the German leader, Adolf Hitler.

# 1941

May 27     **Royal Navy sinks the *Bismarck***
December 2     **German troops freeze in Russian winter**
December 7     **Japanese bomb Pearl Harbor**

## Germans invade Russia

**October 26, Moscow, USSR** In June, Hitler attacked the USSR. Three million troops with 3000 tanks crossed the Russian border. The Russian leader, Stalin, ordered people to burn or destroy anything that would be useful to the Germans including crops, animals and machines. The Germans are now moving towards the capital of the USSR, Moscow. But rain has made all the roads very muddy. The Germans are struggling to keep moving forwards.

## Germans freeze in Russian winter

**December 2, Moscow, USSR** The German army is freezing in the cold Russian winter. Russian troops are now attacking the Germans and forcing them to go back.

## The war at sea

**May 27, North Atlantic Ocean** The Royal Navy sank the huge German battleship the *Bismarck* today. The *Bismarck* had attacked many of the ships that carried food and other supplies from America to Britain.

△ A painting called *The End of the Bismarck* by Charles E. Turner

# Attack at Pearl Harbor

**December 7, Honolulu, Hawaii** In a surprise attack, Japanese planes have bombed American ships at Pearl Harbor in Hawaii. The bombs killed over 2000 people. The USA and Britain have declared war on Japan.

△ Japanese planes attack American ships at Pearl Harbor.

# War in the desert

**April 11, Libya** Earlier this year troops from Britain and other friendly countries (called the Allies) advanced against the Italian army in North Africa. Now German soldiers have taken over from the Italian army. The Germans are attacking the Allied troops fiercely.

# Germans retreat in Africa

**December 10, Libya** The Allies are fighting back against the German army. They have pushed the Germans back to where they were in April.

# The Japanese advance

**December 25, Hong Kong** Japanese forces have landed in Thailand, Malaya and the Philippines. They now control the American island of Guam in the Pacific Ocean. Today the Japanese have also taken Hong Kong.

# Women at work

**December 30, Britain** Women are doing the jobs left by male workers who have gone to fight in the war. The government first asked women to help in March. Now, some women are working in factories, others are working on farms. Many women have also joined the armed forces. They have to work very hard, but are glad to help. Many women have never done this kind of work before.

△ Women workers on the farms are called land girls.

# News in brief . . .

## Amy Johnson missing

**January 8, London, England**
Amy Johnson is missing. People think she may have drowned in the Thames when her plane crashed. Amy Johnson became famous when she flew on her own from Britain to Australia before the war.

## First boy scout dies

**January 8, London, England**
Lord Baden Powell has died. He was 83 years old. Lord Baden Powell started the Boy Scouts in 1908 and the Girl Guides in 1910.

## Comfort in the Underground

**February 28, London, England** Conditions have improved for people in the Underground. Every night people shelter in Underground stations from the bombs. Now the government has put in bunk beds for people to sleep on. Some stations have cookers and kettles for people to make food and drinks.

# Britain and America sign agreement

**August 14, London, England** President Roosevelt and Prime Minister Churchill have held a secret meeting at sea. They signed an agreement to continue fighting until they beat their enemies. The agreement is called the Atlantic Charter.

△ Roosevelt and Churchill meet on board HMS *Prince of Wales*.

# The Blitz in London

**May 31, London, England** The German bombing of London is called the Blitz. In the Blitz, bombs have damaged nearly four million houses in Britain and destroyed about 200,000 more. Many thousands of people have no home.

▽ Many houses have been damaged in the Blitz.

# 1942

## RAF bombs Cologne

**May 31, Cologne, Germany** More than a thousand RAF planes have dropped bombs on the city of Cologne. The bombs destroyed most of the city.

## Germans in Stalingrad

**November 23, Stalingrad, USSR** German troops have been in Stalingrad since August and are dying of hunger and cold. Most of the city is in ruins.

△ Ruined houses in Stalingrad

△ Ruins in the centre of the city

△ The Russians left their guns behind.

△ German troops advance

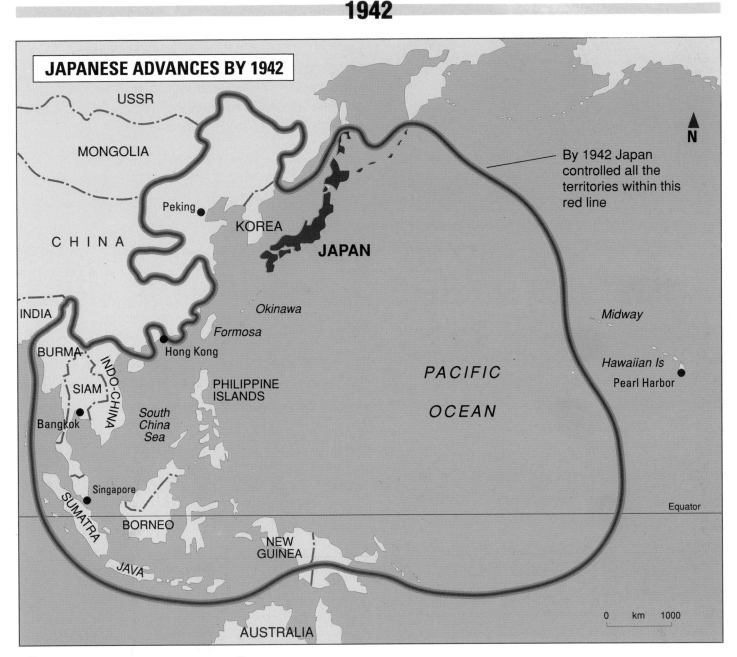

**JAPANESE ADVANCES BY 1942**

By 1942 Japan controlled all the territories within this red line

# Japan marches on

**May 10, Philippine Islands** The Japanese army has had many successes in the Pacific and southeast Asia. The Japanese control Singapore and the Philippines. Now they are threatening India.

# British win in Africa

**November 2, Cairo, Egypt** The British have won a ten-day battle against the Germans at El Alamein in Africa. Under their new commander, General Montgomery, British troops are now chasing the German troops as they retreat westwards.

▽ General Montgomery (centre)

# 1943

## German army retreats

**December 31, USSR**  The German army is retreating from Russia. The Germans have not been able to defeat the Russian army. The Russian army stopped the Germans from capturing Kursk in July. Then the Russians took the city of Kiev from the Germans. Now the Germans are retreating. The Russians are driving the enemy out of their country. So far they have pushed the Germans back 300 kilometres.

## Victory in North Africa

**May 13, Tunisia**  The Allied troops have won a victory in North Africa. The German forces were trapped by the Allies and have given up.

## Invasion of Italy

**September 3, Messina, Italy**  The British army and its Allies have landed in southern Italy. They are fighting the German army in Italy. The government of Italy wants to make peace with the Allies.

△ The British army cross the Sangro River in Italy.

# The war against Japan

**December 29, Solomon Islands, Pacific Ocean**   The Americans are slowly capturing the islands around Japan. But the Japanese soldiers fight until they are killed. They do not give up. Many Americans have also died.

# Allies fight on in Italy

**December 31, Italy**   The American and British armies are still fighting the Germans in Italy. The Germans are fighting very fiercely. The Allies have reached a line of German defences across Italy. This is called the Gustav Line. Progress has been very slow, and the Gustav Line has stopped the Allies advancing any further.

# Allied leaders meet in Persia

**November 28, Tehran, Persia**   The three leaders of the Allied forces are meeting in Persia. They are planning what to do next in the war.

△ Stalin, Roosevelt and Churchill in Persia

# Germans attack ghetto

**June 30, Warsaw, Poland**   On April 19, German troops attacked the Jewish ghetto in Warsaw. The ghetto is the part of the city where the Germans made all the Jewish people live. Now the Germans are taking the Jews to concentration camps. About 7000 Jews have died fighting the Germans.

▷ German troops force Polish Jews out of the ghetto in Warsaw.

# Plans for peace

**September 16, Quebec, Canada** The Allies are planning a better world when the war is over. President Roosevelt and Prime Minister Churchill have agreed to start a new organisation for keeping the world at peace. It will be called the United Nations Organisation.

# Paris is free

**August 26, Paris, France** Paris is free. The Allied troops have forced the Germans to leave. French soldiers were the first to enter the city. People cheered and waved as General Charles de Gaulle led the troops.

△ General Charles de Gaulle in Paris

# The war in Italy

**December 9, Rimini, Italy** The Allied forces have pushed the Germans into northern Italy. But many Allied troops are now leaving Italy and going to fight on the borders of Germany.

# Thousands killed in Warsaw

**October 9, Warsaw, Poland** It is thought that the Germans have killed 200,000 Polish people in Warsaw. The Poles tried to attack the Germans. But the Germans killed the Poles and destroyed all the buildings in Warsaw.

△ The ruins of Warsaw

# Russian victories

**December 1, Belgrade, Yugoslavia** The Russian army has had many victories this year. The Russians have beaten the Germans in Romania, Bulgaria, Hungary and Yugoslavia. As the Germans have left, the Russians have put in their own rulers in these countries. These rulers are controlled by the Soviet government in Moscow. The Russians are quickly building up a new Soviet empire.

# 1945

May 1        Hitler kills himself
May 8        Germany surrenders; VE Day
August 7     Atomic bomb dropped on Hiroshima
August 15    Japan surrenders

## Allies cross the Rhine

**March 31, River Rhine, Germany** American, British and Canadian troops have crossed the River Rhine in Germany. They are about to meet up with troops from the Russian army. The Allied and Russian armies will attack the Germans. The war in Europe is about to end.

## Battles in Berlin

**April 24, Berlin, Germany** The Russian army has reached the German capital, Berlin. The Russians have surrounded the city. Hitler is hiding in an underground shelter somewhere in the city. Hitler still thinks that Germany can win the war. He is still giving orders to his armies. But he has only a million men to defend Berlin. Many are young boys, others are old men. The German airforce, the Luftwaffe, no longer exists.

△ The Russian flag flies in Berlin over the Reichstag, the parliament building.

## Hitler is dead

**May 1, Berlin, Germany** Hitler is dead. He killed himself yesterday in his underground shelter in Berlin. The Italian leader, Mussolini, is also dead. He was shot three days ago.

## Germany surrenders

**May 8, Rheims, France** The German leaders have surrendered to General Eisenhower in Rheims. The war in Europe is over. But the war with Japan continues.

△ A survivor from the Belsen concentration camp

# London celebrates victory

**May 8, London, England**  Today is Victory in Europe Day. It is called VE Day for short. The centre of London is full of people singing, dancing and cheering. The royal family stood on the balcony at Buckingham Palace this afternoon. They waved to the crowds of cheering people below. In Whitehall Prime Minister Churchill came out to see the crowd. The people sang 'For He's a Jolly Good Fellow' to him.

△ Celebrations in London on VE day

# Inside the Belsen concentration camp

**April 15, Belsen, Germany**  When the first Allied soldiers went into the concentration camps in Germany they were horrified by what they saw. Many thousands of Jewish people died in the concentration camps. This is how one soldier described what he saw:

"About 35,000 corpses were reckoned, more actually than the living. Of the living, there were about 30,000 . . .

The camp was so full because people had been brought here from east and west. Some people were brought from Nordhausen, a five-day journey, without food. Many had marched for two or three days. There was no food at all in the camp, a few piles of roots (vegetables) – amidst the piles of dead bodies. Some of the dead bodies were of people so hungry that though the roots were guarded by SS-men they had tried to storm them and had been shot down. There was no water. . ."

(Derek Sington, political officer,
reported by
Patrick Gordon-Walker
in *Book of Reportage*, Faber 1987)

# The forgotten war

**May 19, Thailand** British and Indian troops have driven the Japanese out of India and Burma. They are now about to invade Thailand. The British and Indian forces are led by General 'Bill' Slim. But in Europe many people have forgotten about the war in these countries. The papers have only written about the struggles in Europe and the Pacific.

# Hiroshima destroyed

**August 7, Washington, USA** The Americans have dropped a new kind of bomb on the city of Hiroshima in Japan. An American B29 Superfortress plane dropped the bomb yesterday. It exploded with a huge, purple ball of fire. A dark cloud, shaped like a mushroom, rose from the bomb. This was an atomic bomb. It destroyed the city of Hiroshima. The bomb killed and injured thousands of people. The American President, Harry S. Truman, has threatened Japan with more atomic bombs unless it surrenders.

# Japan surrenders

**August 15, Tokyo, Japan** On August 9, the Americans dropped another atomic bomb. It fell on Nagasaki in Japan and killed thousands of people. The Emperor of Japan has surrendered. This means that World War II is finally over.

△ Hiroshima after the bomb

# Death in Hiroshima

**September 9, Hiroshima, Japan** This is a description of what happened when the atomic bomb dropped on Hiroshima: "Within a few seconds the thousands of people in the streets and the gardens in the centre of the town were scorched by a wave of searing heat. Many were killed instantly, others lay writhing on the ground screaming in agony from the intolerable pain of their burns. Trams were picked up and tossed aside as though they had neither weight nor solidity. Trains were flung off the rails as though they were toys. Horses, dogs and cattle suffered the same fate as human beings. Even the vegetation did not escape."

(Marcel Junod,
*Warrior without Weapons*,
Jonathan Cape 1951)

# News in brief . . .

## President dies suddenly

**April 12, Washington, USA**
President Roosevelt died suddenly today. The Vice-President Harry S. Truman will become the new president of the United States.

## Lights shine in Britain

**July 15, London, England**
The blackout in Britain is over. During the blackout no lights were allowed at night in the streets, in shops or in buildings. The blackout made it more difficult for German planes to see where towns and cities were. Now streets and shops are lit up again.

▷ Clement Attlee, the leader of the Labour party

## Countries work for peace

**October 24, New York, USA**
Twenty-nine countries have signed the United Nations Charter. This is an agreement to try to prevent war in the future.

▷ The symbol of the new United Nations.

## Labour party win election

**July 26, London, England**
The Labour party has won the British election. The leader of the Labour party is Clement Attlee.

# Germany and Berlin split up

**August 2, Potsdam, Germany**
The Allies are splitting Germany up. Different countries will control different areas of Germany. Leaders of the Allied countries are meeting at Potsdam. They have decided that Russia will take over the eastern half of Germany. The Americans, the British and the French will run the rest of the country. The German capital, Berlin, will be divided into four parts.

## The United Nations

**January 10, London, England** Today the United Nations is holding its first meeting. The Foreign Minister from Belgium, Paul Henri Spaak, will be the President of the United Nations. He was elected by one vote. The United States and the countries in the West voted for him. The USSR and the countries of the East wanted a different President. The countries of the West and East do not trust each other. This is very different to when they were Allies in the war.

## Nazi leaders put on trial

**September 30, Nuremberg, Germany** The wartime Allies have put the Nazi leaders on trial. The trial is being held in Nuremberg, Germany. Eleven Nazi leaders have been sentenced to death. Eight will be put in prison.

## Goering escapes hanging

**October 16, Nuremberg, Germany** Ten Nazi leaders were hanged this morning. But one of the leaders, Hermann Goering, escaped hanging. He killed himself by eating a poisonous pill.

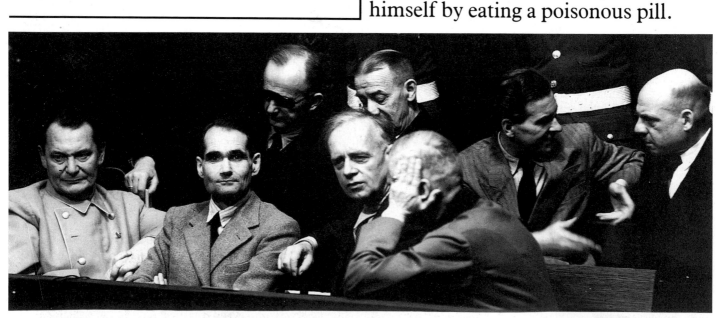

△ Nazi leaders on trial at Nuremberg

# Iron Curtain falls

**March 5, Fulton, USA** The countries of the East and the West are separating into two groups. These groups are often called 'blocs'. The Eastern bloc is controlled by the Communist government in the USSR. Eastern bloc countries include the USSR, Hungary Bulgaria, Romania, Poland, Czechoslovakia, Yugoslavia and the eastern part of Germany (see map). The East and West do not trust each other. Sir Winston Churchill has described the division between the two blocs as an 'Iron Curtain'.

"A shadow has fallen upon the scenes so lately lighted by the Allied victory . . . From Stettin on the Baltic to Trieste on the Adriatic, an iron curtain has descended across Europe."

# The United Nations bans the bomb

**December 14, New York, USA** All the members of the United Nations have voted to ban the atomic bomb. The United Nations want to prevent another atomic explosion like the ones at Hiroshima and Nagasaki.

▽ An atomic explosion

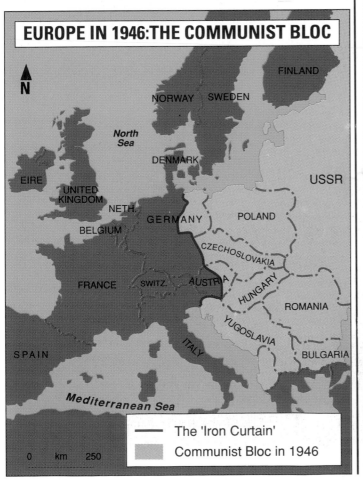

**EUROPE IN 1946: THE COMMUNIST BLOC**

N

FINLAND
NORWAY  SWEDEN
North Sea
DENMARK
EIRE
UNITED KINGDOM
NETH.
GERMANY  POLAND
BELGIUM
CZECHOSLOVAKIA
USSR
FRANCE  SWITZ.  AUSTRIA
HUNGARY
ROMANIA
YUGOSLAVIA
SPAIN
ITALY
BULGARIA
Mediterranean Sea

— The 'Iron Curtain'
▨ Communist Bloc in 1946

0   km   250

# PEOPLE OF THE 30s AND 40s

### Neville Chamberlain 1869–1940

Neville Chamberlain was the British Prime Minister when Britain entered the war in 1939. Chamberlain tried to persuade Hitler not to go to war. But Hitler fooled Chamberlain with his promises about Czechoslovakia (see page 18). In 1940, Chamberlain resigned and Winston Churchill took his place as Prime Minister. Chamberlain died of cancer in 1940.

### Franklin D. Roosevelt 1882–1945

Franklin D. Roosevelt was President of the United States from 1933 to 1945. He led the United States into World War II in 1941. In 1944 he was elected President for the fourth time. He died in 1945, just before the war ended.

### Walt Disney 1901–1966

Walt Disney was an American film-maker. Many of his films were cartoons. He invented Mickey Mouse, Minnie Mouse, Donald Duck, Goofy, Pluto and many other characters.

### Francisco Franco 1892–1975

Francisco Franco was the leader of Spain from 1937 until 1975. He organised the attack on the government which started the Spanish Civil War.

### Adolf Hitler 1889–1945

Adolf Hitler was born in Austria, but he moved to Germany. He became leader of Germany in 1933. He ordered the invasions of Czechoslovakia, Austria and Poland. World War II followed. He killed himself in 1945, as the Russians entered Berlin.

### Benito Mussolini 1883–1945

Benito Mussolini was the leader of Italy. Before this Mussolini was a teacher, then a journalist. He was on Hitler's side in World War II. But the Allies beat him in 1943. Mussolini was shot and killed in 1945.

### Joseph Stalin 1879–1953

Joseph Stalin was the leader of the revolution in Russia in 1917. Millions of people died on his orders. In World War II, Stalin led Russia to victory over the Germans.